A working guide to GROWING THROUGH DIVORCE

Jim Smoke
Lisa Guest

HARVEST HOUSE PUBLISHERS
Eugene, Oregon 97402

Verses marked NASB are taken from the New American Standard Bible, © The Lockman Foundation 1960, 1962, 1963, 1968, 1971, 1972, 1973, 1975, 1977. Used by permission.

Verses marked NIV are taken from the Holy Bible, New International Version, Copyright © 1978 by the New York International Bible Society. Used by permission.

Verses marked NKJV are taken from the Holy Bible, New King James Version, Copyright © 1979, 1980, 1982 by Thomas Nelson, Inc. Used by permission.

Verses marked Phillips are taken from The New Testament in Modern English, Revised Edition, J.B. Phillips, Translator. © J.B. Phillips 1958, 1960, 1972. Used by permission of Macmillan Publishing Co., Inc.

Verses marked RSV are taken from the Revised Standard Version of the Bible, Copyright 1946, 1952, © 1971, 1973 by the National Council of the Churches of Christ in the U.S.A. Used by permission.

Verses marked TLB are taken from The Living Bible, Copyright 1971 by Tyndale House Publishers, Wheaton, Illinois. Used by permission.

Selections from *Every Single Day* are written and copyrighted © 1983 by Jim Smoke. Used by permission of Fleming H. Revell Company.

A WORKING GUIDE for GROWING THROUGH DIVORCE

Copyright © 1985 by Harvest House Publishers
Eugene, Oregon 97402

ISBN 0-89081-477-5

All rights reserved. No portion of this book may be reproduced in any form without the written permission of the Publisher.

Printed in the United States of America.

Contents

Introduction 5
How to Use This Guide 9
1. Is This Really Happening to Me?.............. 11
2. Letting Go.................................. 17
3. Getting Your Ex-Spouse in Focus 25
4. Assuming Responsibility for Myself 31
5. Assuming Responsibility for My Children 37
6. Assuming Responsibility for My Future 47
7. Finding a Family 57
8. Finding and Experiencing Forgiveness 63
9. Thirty-Seven Going on Seventeen 69
10. Remarriage—Yours, Mine, and Maybe Our Families' 77
11. How I've Grown 85
12. Practical Pointers, How to Help, and One Last Word 89

Introduction

We've all experienced the kind of day that flies by with a flurry of activity and accomplishment, energy and enthusiasm. We've also experienced the seemingly endless day when minutes move with the speed of a glacier and we wonder if dinnertime will ever come. When a person goes through the process of a divorce, chances are that he or she has more slow days than swift days, days that drag instead of soar. This pace characterizes the "I'll-grit-my-teeth-and-somehow-survive" attitude behind the statement "I'm going through a divorce right now." Each day presents itself as another mountain to climb; each day seems another endurance race with at best only a shadowy finish line.

As the title of my book suggests, I want to propose an alternative to this. I want to help you *grow* through divorce. I want to help you receive each day as a unique gift, with new lessons to be learned, new healing to be found, and new steps to be taken. As you read through this manual, you'll get to know the person you are—and you'll come to like him or her! You'll have the chance to let God help you grow through divorce, and you'll come to know His tender and healing love. You'll also set goals for yourself, and you'll achieve them. Before you begin, let me share with you some specific goals I have for myself as I write this manual.

I want to encourage you to be honest with yourself.

Just as defining a problem helps us solve it, or identifying the enemy leads to victory, being honest with ourselves about our thoughts, feelings, hurts, and fears allows us to heal and grow. Honesty is the means by which we define the problem (Are you too comfortable with your pain? Are you hiding behind the mask of "hurting person"?) and identify the enemy (Are you angry? Bitter? Frightened? Lonely?). Upon taking these steps of honesty, you can deal with the situation, which you now see more clearly. As I said in the *How to Survive a Divorce* tapes, the greatest help you can get is the help you give yourself. Honesty may often be difficult, but it is an essential tonic for the growth which you give yourself.

I want to help you deal with the battle of your head versus your heart.

If you haven't noticed already, an ongoing battle between your head and your heart can slow down your healing process. All too often the feelings of the heart undermine the thoughts of the head—those rational ideas which can help you deal with reality and therefore help you move ahead. Emotions can override logical decisions and can distract you from circumstances which need your careful attention. God has made us both feeling and thinking people, and we need to strive for balance between our emotions and our ideas.

I want to motivate you to find a community for support and healing.

This goal may not be very appealing right now as you deal with the feelings of rejection inherent in a divorce. Why would you want to take the risk of once again being hurt? But this risk usually pays off. I've seen in my experience that strong people ask for help. They make themselves open to new friendships, and they are stronger people because of it. Start slowly, but do start. A trusted friend can make this difficult time easier for you, and a trusted friend is the beginning of a community that will keep you from feeling alone.

I want to offer you the anchors of hope and of affirmation about who you are.

Like many people, I have found Jesus Christ to be the surest foundation for this kind of self-acceptance, self-confidence, and hope for the future. You may already have found in Him these things as well as the guidance, peace, and comfort which He freely gives to those who follow Him. If you do not yet know Jesus, my references to Him and His love for you may be just the introduction you need. Remember, strong people ask for help, and wise people turn to Jesus, who said, "Come to Me, all you who labor and are heavy laden, and I will give you rest (Matthew 11:28 NKJV).

How am I going to achieve these goals? How am I going to help you grow through your divorce? By focusing on three different aspects of growth—sowing, tending, and reaping.

Sowing

I will be sowing seeds of hope and healing from my devotional book *Every Single Day* (Fleming H. Revell, 1983). These thoughts will be based on a verse or brief passage from Scripture. We will look to the Bible for valuable insights and practical guidelines.

I will also be reintroducing ideas from the *Growing Through Divorce* text, ideas which are further discussed in the *How to Survive a Divorce* tapes. I want to encourage you to listen to the tapes. That's an effective way to reinforce for yourself the ideas you find in the text.

Tending

First, look at yourself. Do you see ground that is fertile and able to sustain new growth? More than likely you'll have to get rid of some rocks and weeds. Second, think about how my ideas apply to your particular situation. Would you like to grow? Could the points I make help you grow? Grab the handles I offer and hang on to the ideas I present. In the "Tending" sections, you'll clear the ground for growth and nourish ideas I've sown. (I also want to encourage you to answer the questions at the end of each chapter in *Growing Through Divorce*. Those questions will help you consider important issues from a slightly different perspective.)

Reaping

When seeds are planted and well cared for, growth results. You'll be given the chance in these sections to note your movement forward. You will find a space to record a positive step you have already taken that day or that week. Complementing that notation of progress will be this section's goal-setting and the opportunity to focus your energy in worthwhile directions. While some goals will be easier to define and achieve than others, each goal will help you notice the growth that is happening in your life.

P.S.

The initials P.S. mean "postscript"—an afterthought well worth mentioning. In this book, each chapter will have room for a P.S. This space is for you to record the feelings, hurts, struggles, memories, and hopes you are dealing with at the moment. As you work through this guide, and then go back and read past postscripts, you will see these initials start to mean "Positive Steps." These postscripts will stand as concrete evidence of the growth that is happening in your life.

Finally, as every gardener knows, growth can be inhibited by various factors. I want to mention an important one now: Other people can unintentionally slow down your healing process. Be aware that people may seem (or actually be) insensitive, for a variety of reasons.

— People don't understand what you're feeling because they haven't experienced it themselves.
— People don't know what to say or how to help, so they simply avoid you.
— People are dealing with their own feelings of hurt that resulted from your divorce.
— People are threatened: Divorce is often thought of as being contagious, and they don't want to be the next ones to suffer.

These are just four reasons why people you had always relied upon may seem distant or unhelpful or cold right now. Give them the benefit of the doubt, and then give them time. Give them the chance to work through their own feelings, to adjust to your new situation, and to define a working relationship with you. In the meantime, find new friends who can understand, who do know how to help, who can offer compassion and support, and who are not threatened by your situation or your pain. These people do exist, and they can be an important part of your healing process.

One more thing. Just as I advised giving your friends time, I want to advise you to give yourself time too. Don't baby yourself, but do be patient with yourself. Growth—of a tomato plant or a tree, of a child or an adult—happens a little at a time. Growth happens a day at a time as we face the decisions, experiences, and hurdles of a given 24-hour period. You grow a little each day even if you can't see it or feel it. You may not always be able to greet the morning with the exultant words of the psalmist, "This is the day which the Lord has made; we will rejoice and be glad in it" (Psalm 118:24 NKJV), but you can still close the day with thanks to Him for caring about the details of your life, for walking with you as you deal with them, and for promising to be with you tomorrow.

How to Use This Guide

By Yourself

When you pick up this book, pick up a pen or pencil as well! The book is designed for you to *use*, not just to read—and a pen will encourage you to do more than just read the words. Your answer does not need to be long. Don't worry about sentence structure or correct spelling. The book is not a test! The book is an opportunity for you to think about some issues in your life, to face the emotions which may be hiding inside you, and to get to know yourself a little better. The more thought and the more effort you put into your answers, the more growth you'll experience.

With a Group

If you are a small-group leader, let this guide to *Growing Through Divorce* be a resource tool as you design your 12-week divorce-recovery workshop. As you plan your weekly meetings, consider the following suggestions.

In your discussion times, emphasize the "Sowing" and "Reaping" sections. The "Sowing" sections are a time of Bible study. The power of God's Word can heal, encourage, challenge, instruct, and comfort. Let that power be released into your group by spending time studying the passages which introduce each lesson. The "Reaping" sections allow a family spirit to develop within your group. People will reach out to one another as they hold each other accountable to goals they set. Friendships will develop as they struggle to reach those goals, as they discuss goals not yet achieved, and as they celebrate goals that they meet.

Let the "Tending" sections be done privately, at least at the beginning of the workshop series. People who are experiencing a divorce are emotionally raw and vulnerable. Be sensitive to this, and don't force your group members to share when they aren't yet ready to. As they get to know each other better, choose questions from the "Tending" sections which you feel are appropriate for group discussion, and include these in your meeting time.

The best guideline I can offer is this: *Be sensitive.* Get to know your group—both the individuals and the personality of the group as a whole. Be aware of the participants' moods, hurts, and questions. Strive to know when and how much to push. Make yourself available on a one-to-one basis. Be able to suggest professional counselors and psychologists for those who are interested.

Pray for the individuals in your group. This guide, the book, and your group are tools which our healing God can use. It is the tool of prayer, however, which will release that power into people's lives like no meeting or book can do by itself.

Chapter 1

Is This Really Happening To Me?

Sowing

"The Lord is close to the brokenhearted and saves those who are crushed in spirit" (Psalm 34:18 NIV).

• Do you feel that God is standing close to you or far away from you right now?

If you are feeling isolated, broken, and discouraged, consider how God can save you from this.

> Sometimes He has to save us from ourselves and our self-inflicted wounds. It is easy to blame ourselves when we are down, and lock our spirits inside the prison of self-pity.
>
> At other times, He has to rescue us from those around us who appear to help but in reality hinder. He brings us back to a basic trust in Him alone.
>
> In the last area, God saves us from situations that can damage us further. He moves us into new and safer places (*Every Single Day*, p. 42).

God does stand close. Can you feel that closeness today?

• Which feeling best describes your situation right now?

        Blame   Self-pity   Trust in God

• Even if you can't *feel* God's closeness, *choose* to believe that He is near. Choose to believe His promise to stand by you. Follow up the question "Is this really happening to me?" with Psalm

34:18, Psalm 46:1, Romans 8:31, or Deuteronomy 31:8.

Tending

Now let's get more in touch with the feelings you may have right now. Put a checkmark next to those emotions you are experiencing. This kind of acknowledgment is an important part of being honest with yourself, a point I emphasized in my opening letter to you.

_____ Shocked	_____ Bitter	_____ Vindictive
_____ Angry	_____ Hateful	_____ Betrayed
_____ Dazed	_____ Empty	_____ Numb
_____ Hostile	_____ Cheated	_____ Other _____

You probably checked more than one emotion—and such emotional chaos is normal. Repeat this aloud: "Emotions are normal. My emotions are natural." (Throughout this guide I'll ask you to say aloud such positive statements. The word "freedom" will be your cue to say the sentence aloud and so declare its truth. The purpose is to reinforce ideas which are affirming, healing, and freeing.)

Generally the first stage that divorcing people experience is *shock*. And shock manifests itself in various ways. Which of these things have you found yourself doing?

- _____ Retreating into yourself.
- _____ Denying what is happening.
- _____ Refusing to talk about the divorce.
- _____ Withdrawing from friends and social contacts.
- _____ Moving to a new home.
- _____ Changing jobs.
- _____ Struggling with a sense of failure.
- _____ Battling an intense feeling of guilt.
- _____ Transferring your anger to an innocent party.
- _____ Telling everyone—anyone who will listen—all the details of your situation.
- _____ Keeping up a frantic social life.
- _____ Hiding behind a busy schedule.
- _____ Clinging to hope that is based more in fantasy than in reality.

If you aren't sure about the wisdom of the hope you're nursing, review the questions on pages 16 and 17 in the text and remember to be honest with yourself.

Whatever behaviors you placed a checkmark by, these behaviors may be fading. The shock may be starting to wear off and you may find yourself *adjusting* somewhat to your new situation. As I wrote in the text, shock is accepting the facts of divorce and adjusting is doing something about it. Consider these possibilities.

1. Positive mourning. Which of the following statements can you say aloud as an act of self-emancipation?

    ____ I'm glad I had the good times and I wish I still had them.
    ____ I'm sorry that the good times are gone now, but I know that there is still much happiness left for me in life.
    ____ I have the human right to feel loss, grief, and sorrow.
    ____ I hurt, and for now there is an empty space in my life.

2. Negative mourning. Which of these statements remind you of yourself?

    ____ I feel as if I'm sinking in a sea of self-pity.
    ____ I feel that the end of the marriage was all my fault.
    ____ I feel that the end of the marriage was all my ex-spouse's fault.
    ____ I feel that life has dealt me a bad hand, and I'm going to let everyone know it!

3. Assembling the pieces. How is your life right now like a jigsaw puzzle?

What pieces of your life are most difficult for you to work with?

    ____ Sense of disorganization to life.
    ____ Extreme emotional highs and lows.
    ____ Loneliness.
    ____ Being a single parent.
    ____ Looking for a job.
    ____ Deciding where to live.
    ____ Struggling to explain the situation to family (kids included) and friends.
    ____ Other:_____.

This time of tending has been a time of evaluation. Since growth happens only when conditions are right, it is important to know what the conditions of your life are. Again, acknowledgment and honesty with yourself provide fertile ground for growth. The crucial step, however, involves making a choice.

Reaping

• Today I could say aloud with a degree of confidence the following statement of positive mourning:

• This week I will carry with me the following idea and so strive to keep my mourning from inhibiting my growth:

• This week I will limit my time for feeling sorry for myself to:

_____ 30 seconds   _____ 15 seconds   _____ 10 seconds

Note that the preceding three instructions involve choices. You can choose one or the other from each of the following pairs:

Hating yourself	or	Learning to like yourself.
Refusing to believe you'll survive	or	Believing not that you'll merely survive, but that you'll emerge healthier and stronger than before.
Thinking of divorce as negative and self-defeating	or	Looking at divorce as an experience which can help you grow.
Going through divorce	or	Growing through divorce.

What choices are you making in your life? List one or two from above or from the eight "Growing Through Divorce" steps on pages 21 and 22 of the text as reminders of where you're heading.

1)

2)

Now set a few more goals for yourself. Base them on the "Growing Through Divorce" steps which you just reviewed.

• This week I will meet with a healthy person who is struggling but growing. I will spend time with _____.

- I will take time for myself—to think, read, reflect, or meditate. I will spend (how many?) _____ quiet moments on (day?) _____ as a time of rest and renewal.

- Daily I will commit my way to God on this new path. I will begin each morning by:

    ____ Praying.
    ____ Reading the Bible.
    ____ Quietly listening and thinking.
    ____ All of the above.

- This week I will battle a little with the issue of forgiveness. I will have as my weapon the following fact: People rank sins and tend to make divorce the unforgivable one; God does not rank our sins. Instead, He promises to forgive each and every one that we confess (1 John 1:9).

One more time: Are you choosing to *go through* or *grow through* your divorce experience?

FREEDOM: I choose to _____.

P.S.

This space is for sharing what is on your heart and your mind right now. Your words are confidential. Be a good friend to yourself and talk through whatever is bothering you by writing it on paper.

Chapter 2

Letting Go

Sowing

"Be glad for all God is planning for you. Be patient in trouble, and prayerful always" (Romans 12:12 TLB).

• Would you like God to tell you all He is planning for you in the next year or five years?

• Consider the inevitable struggles which lie ahead. How would knowing about these in advance affect you? Would the results be positive or negative?

> God's instruction is simply to be happy for *all* God is planning for us. He is the Architect of our lives and knows what He is doing. His caution to us as He reveals that daily plan is to be patient when the tough times come, and to always be prayerful. Patience and prayer—the dynamic duo of the Christian walk. Both of them reside near the top of the "tough to do" list in our Christian life.
>
> We do not know how God's plans are going to work out for us today. We do know that we can be glad, because God knows exactly what He is doing. We wait patiently and we pray continually. God reveals the process.
>
> The Architect is at work in your life today. Trust Him! (*Every Single Day*, p. 109).

• What evidence of God's wisdom do you find in the world around you?

- How can this evidence influence your trust in God?

- Paul's instruction to the Roman church is instruction for you today: Be patient and pray. Have you tried doing either of these? The *choice* (there's that word again!) is yours. Let me add that, besides helping you be more patient, prayer will allow you to better know the loving Architect of your life.

By definition, moving forward means moving away from something. That "something" tends to be the known, the familiar—and that "something" therefore involves security. Even if the familiar is unhealthy or painful, it is nevertheless comfortable because there are no surprises or breaks in the routine.

- Do you hesitate to let go of old things and exchange them for something new?

- Are you struggling with fear of the unknown?

Let the next section help you see the unknown that lies ahead as less threatening. Let the next section help you anticipate some of the mental, social, physical, and spiritual changes you may experience as you learn to let go of the past and its pain.

Tending

Having acknowledged either some natural reluctance or some understandable hesitation about the transition from "married" to "single," look more closely at each of the four areas of possible growth.

Mental

What attitudes do the following people *seem* to have toward you? (Let me remind you that you are unable to be objective as you answer this question. You are also unable to be sure that your perception is accurate.) What attitude do you have toward them? Be honest. Let out whatever is inside you, and find yourself letting go of this unhealthy baggage.

	Their Attitude Toward Me	My Attitude Toward Them
Ex-Spouse		
Children		
Relatives		
Friends		

Often, first attitudes and reactions are not permanent. People's attitudes change; your attitudes change. Repeat this exercise from time to time and see what happens. Some friends will stand by you, some relatives will be less angry as they come to terms with reality, and some of your own feelings will soften.

Social

Where have you noticed (or where do you anticipate) the toughest transition from being married to being single?

   ____ Job/career:
   ____ School/education:
   ____ Church/religion:
   ____ Community involvement:
   ____ Lifestyle:
   ____ Support system of friends:

Be specific. The power of a fear or struggle becomes less once we acknowledge what we are up against.

FREEDOM: I have to face some changes and probably some discrimination in my social life, but none of this is a commentary on my value as a person.

Physical

- At what point during your daily routine do you most notice the absence of your former spouse?

- What can you do to ease the sting of that moment? Be creative!

Can you rearrange your routine? Can you call a friend? Can you call on God?

> **FREEDOM:** Being alone right now is not a life sentence imposed as a penalty for my divorce.

Spiritual

- Is your divorce driving you *away from God* or *toward God?*

- If you answered "away from God," consider these things:
  - God made you an emotional person. It's okay to be angry—even angry at God.
  - Don't confuse your church with God. He is more acceptting of us than other people are.
  - Don't stay away from God because you feel that your divorce is an unforgivable sin. God doesn't rank sins!

- If you answered "toward God," you have beside you the greatest Caretaker. He will sow seeds of growth and see them through to harvesttime.

> **FREEDOM:** God forgives me even when people around me don't seem able to, and this forgiving God is the Author of new beginnings.

Reaping

This lesson's four statements of freedom were four statements about letting go—

- of responsibility for other people's thoughts and feelings.
- of feeling worthless and unable to have healthy relationships.
- of the troubling illusion that you'll be lonely forever.
- of the idea that God cannot or will not forgive you for your divorce.

Now we'll focus on reaching out and replacing those life-draining ways with life-giving goals. First, though, be aware of the choice you're making.

FREEDOM: I am choosing to let go of old things and replace them with new things.

Now say aloud, "I am divorced. I am single. I am okay." How easy was that?

_____
Painless   Difficult

Do this weekly and note your progress as you face reality more directly.

Mental

One positive mental effort this week was:

This week I gave (whom?) _____ the benefit of the doubt when he/she seemed cold and uncaring.

This week I will remember (write the freedom statement which is most appealing to you right now):

Social

One positive social encounter this week was when:

This week I will initiate some social activity by—

- _____ striking up a conversation with the boss.
- _____ investigating other career paths.
- _____ talking to a professor/teacher after class about the lecture.
- _____ calling up someone from church whom I've always wanted to get to know better.
- _____ attending a meeting of the local _____ (choose a community group!).
- _____ being a friend to _____ instead of waiting for someone to be a friend to me.
- _____ being a good friend to myself by cooking something special or taking myself out to dinner.

Physical

This week, on (day) _____ at (time) _____, I noticed that the physical absence of my former mate didn't bother me as much as it once did.

This week I will compensate for the physical absence by—

Spiritual

One positive sign of spiritual health from this week was:

This week I will try to improve my relationship with God by—

Review the list of "Keys to Accepting a New Identity" on page 31 of the text. Now set goals for yourself.

Key 2: This week I will create a "new experience in living" by—

Key 3: At least once this week I will break out my mold of—

____ mother/father.
____ employee/employer.
____ other: _____.
   by _____
_____.

Key 6: This week I will act on my freedom to fail. I will take a risk and try_____. If I fail, I'll learn something from the experience.

FREEDOM: I can let go of the past, grab on to exciting new things today, and so grow toward the future. This process will take time—and I will allow whatever time it takes because I'm worth that investment.

P.S.

Chapter 3

Getting Your Ex-Spouse In Focus

Sowing

"How tremendous is the power available to us who believe in God" (Ephesians 1:19,20 Phillips).

• Do you believe in God?

• Are you tapping into the power that He offers to us as His people?

> Knowing God's power is ready for us to claim in all situations gives us the strength to face life's daily conflicts and problems. It does not do us any good, however, if we never use it. It is like being a millionaire and living in poverty. You have to use what is available to you or it will do you no good.
>
> All of God's power is ready for us to plug into: power to live, power to meet frustrations, power to know the right decisions, power to make the necessary changes in our lives that will help us grow.
>
> Are you tapping into God's power in your daily life? Try it today. You will be surprised at the results! (*Every Single Day*, p. 53).

• In what daily situations would you like to experience God's power?

- How are you tapping into that divine power source? Through prayer? Trust? Study? Meditation?

- Choose one hurdle that you are currently facing, and ask for God's involvement—for His guidance and His peace as well as His power.

It is quite likely that you listed as a daily situation which could be helped by God's power "dealing with my former spouse." That's the hurdle we'll be looking at in this lesson.

- How do you feel about your ex-spouse right now?

_____ Hostile	_____ Betrayed	_____ Vengeful
_____ Full of pity	_____ Angry	_____ Hurt
_____ Humiliated	_____ Bitter	_____ Other: _____

Tending

Chances are that your feelings toward your former mate are rooted in whatever caused your divorce. Review the list below and look again at pages 36-38 of the text for a description of each cause. Write a brief definition of each type listed.

1) The "Victim" Divorce

2) The "Problem" Divorce

3) The "Little Boy, Little Girl" Divorce

4) The "I Was Conned" Divorce

5) The "Shotgun" Divorce

6) The "Menopause" Divorce

7) The "No-Fault" Divorce

Which of the seven causes most closely describes your divorce?

We aren't going to dwell on the reasons or events or circumstances which led to your divorce. While it is wise and necessary to look at some of that—it helps you accept the reality of your situation—too much looking back only prevents growth. We are therefore going to look at five guidelines to help you get your ex-spouse in a healthier focus—healthier for *you*.

1. Take the detachment one day at a time.

- This is not the first time you've heard this! Is "one day at a time" a wise approach to life? Why or why not?

- Worry removes our focus from the day and from God and instead has us looking toward the future with fear and trembling. Look up Philippians 4:6,7 and write it below as a freedom statement.

FREEDOM: _____
_____
_____
_____

2. Try to make the break as clean as possible.

- Is a clean break a good idea? Why or why not? (I firmly believe that a clean break is the only healthy way to deal with a divorce. Only a clean break will promote your personal growth. Review pages 40-41 for why I am adamant about this.)

- How clean has your break from your spouse been?

_____

| We made the break as | Our lives are still |
| clean as possible. | quite entangled. |

- How are your lives still intertwined?

    ____ We share meals.
    ____ We share babysitting duties.
    ____ We share gardening/cooking/car repair chores.
    ____ We share a sexual relationship.
    ____ We share a dating relationship.
    ____ I use every opportunity to see him/her, even though it's never been an entirely positive experience.

_____ I seem to have forgotten all the bad and so I nurse the hope that we'll get back together.
_____ Other: _____

FREEDOM: I will be happier when I begin to build a new life for myself—and that won't happen as long as I cling to the past.

(What choice is the basis of this freedom?)

3. Quit accepting responsibility for your ex-spouse.

- Which thoughts have concerned you since your divorce?

   _____ Can my former mate make it on his/her own?
   _____ Will he/she commit suicide?
   _____ What if he starves? What if her house and car fall apart?
   _____ What if he/she has a nervous breakdown?
   _____ What if she can't find a job? What if he doesn't send the child support?
   _____ Other: _____

- Are you feeling the desire to take care of your former mate? Is this healthy for you?

- Are you thereby forcing him/her into a state of dependence on you? Is this healthy for him/her? For you?

FREEDOM: Few people learn to stand alone and discover their own resources and abilities *until they have to*.

4. Don't let your children intimidate you.

- How are you feeling because of your children's actions, statements, and attitudes?

_____	Guilty	_____	Frustrated
_____	Like a failure	_____	Empty
_____	Bewildered	_____	Pressured
_____	Misunderstood	_____	Heartbroken
_____	Angry	_____	Other: _____

- What motives are probably behind the things your children do or say right now? Let this understanding help you be more patient with them and less hard on yourself.

FREEDOM: I acknowledge that children cannot always understand adult decisions.

I love my children and will continue to do so even though their behavior hurts me.

I don't need to be intimidated by my children, especially when I remind myself that their behavior stems from their own hurt, confusion, and insecurity.

5. Don't get trapped in your "child" state.

• Which of the following behaviors have you fallen into since your divorce?

    ____ Throwing temper tantrums.
    ____ Wanting to "get even" with your ex-spouse.
    ____ Telling lies.
    ____ Being jealous.
    ____ Fighting over petty things.
    ____ Calling your ex-spouse names.
    ____ Letting the phone ring and then hanging up when he/she answers.
    ____ Spying on your former mate.
    ____ Spreading negative information (whether true or false) among your friends.
    ____ Other: _____

• What does such childish behavior accomplish?

FREEDOM: My growth will happen more easily if my dealings with my ex-spouse are handled under the conditions of a truce rather than a war.

Reaping

• This week I was pleased about the following aspect of my encounter with my ex-spouse:

- Which growth guidelines seem the easiest for you to work on this week?

- Write out one or two specific goals for yourself which will help you follow that guideline.

    1)

    2)

FREEDOM: Everyone benefits when people are treated with respect and dignity. I will begin to treat my ex-spouse in this way. My part of the war is over!

P.S.

Chapter 4

Assuming Responsibility For Myself

Sowing

"O Lord God! You have made the heavens and earth by your great power; nothing is too hard for you!" (Jeremiah 32:17 TLB).

- What else in creation reveals to you God's great power?

> Jeremiah wrote today's words while he was in prison. He was looking beyond the problems Israel faced to its future. He saw disarray and impending defeat all around him. Yet he called forth the reality that the God who made everything by His power still had enough of that power available to meet daily situations. He affirmed that God could handle His own problems as well as those of Israel.
>
> Do you have two lists of problems in your life? One contains the things *you* will handle, and the other the things you want *God* to handle. I suggest that you make one list today and simply give it to God. Then believe that you can't come up with anything that He is not able to take care of (*Every Single Day*, p. 71).

- List those problems or concerns which seem too big for you to handle. Then give the list to God.

- List those things which seem too small and insignificant to bother God with. Give these to God as well.

- If there is anything you're concerned about which isn't on either list, make a third list and—you guessed it—give it to God!

As this lesson will point out, assuming responsibility for yourself does not mean tackling life as the Lone Ranger. It doesn't mean being completely self-sufficient and totally independent of God and of the people He puts into your life to help you. "Assuming responsibility for yourself" is simply another way of saying, "Grow through your divorce." Learn from the experience, learn about yourself, and learn healthful ways to deal with the situations of life.

Tending

- Why is each one of us so ready to blame something or someone else for the circumstances of our life?

- Who are you blaming for your divorce?

___ Spouse	___ Job stress	___ Society's pressures
___ Children	___ Neighborhood	___ Friends' patterns
___ The office flirt	___ The church	___ "We just grew apart."
___ Parents/in-laws	___ Self	___ Other: _____

Whatever or whomever you find to blame, the fact is that the tendency to blame inhibits your growth. Blaming prevents you from understanding yourself and your situation. What's the alternative? Assuming responsibility for yourself. Let's look closely at five areas for potential growth.

1. I assume responsibility for my part of the failure of my marriage.

- How easy is it for you to say the following statement aloud: "I contributed to the failure of my marriage"?

_____

Simple   Difficult

- Why is such a statement difficult to make—if not for you personally, for other people?

Assuming Responsibility for Myself • 33

- Do you have standards of perfection for yourself that not even God has for you?

FREEDOM: I have failed in my marriage—but that does not mean that I am a failure, a person destined to fail at everything I try. I can and will move ahead.

2. I assume responsibility for my present situation.

- Wishing things were different accomplishes nothing. Working toward change is the only solution. Complete the following chart. Think carefully and creatively. I've given you cues in the left-hand column.

	I am responsible for:	I will fulfill this responsibility by:
(As an employee)		
(As a parent)		
(As a homeowner/renter)		
(As a breadwinner)		
(As a jobhunter)		
(As a church member)		

FREEDOM: I can do all things through Christ who strengthens me (Philippians 4:13 NKJV).

3. I assume responsibility for my future.

- Since opening this guide, you've had the chance to set positive goals for yourself. Maybe the goals you've set are few in number or still rather undefined. That's okay. Whatever you have is a start. Work toward clarifying your goals—then work toward achieving them. Remember one wise person's words: "Shoot at nothing and that is what you will hit."

- Jot down two or three goals from whatever facet of your life

34 • Growing Through Divorce

you are most excited about right now. The goals may be mental, social, spiritual, educational, vocational, family-oriented, or designed for personal growth.

FREEDOM: I will instruct you and teach you in the way you should go; I will guide you with My eye (Psalm 32:8 NKJV).

4. I assume responsibility for myself—for my thoughts, feelings, and actions.

Thoughts

• We won't dwell on whatever negative thoughts are haunting you. Instead, I want you to consider the source of those thoughts. Where do you think they come from?

_____ Guilt	_____ Loneliness	_____ Tiredness
_____ Laziness	_____ Fear	_____ Anger

_____ Other people's comments to you
_____ An overactive imagination
_____ Other: _____

• Do you have to give credibility to the source you just identified? *No!* In other words, you can choose not to believe that source and those negative thoughts. You can choose to let go of those destructive ideas and replace them with the words of God and the statements of freedom that you'll find in the Bible and in this guide.

FREEDOM: I can control what I think about.

Feelings

• How are you feeling right now? This will be harder for some of you than it is for others—and that's okay.

_____ Angry	_____ Lonely	_____ Depressed
_____ Afraid	_____ Hopeful	_____ Strong
_____ Calm	_____ Frustrated	_____ Lovable
_____ Guilty	_____ Trusting	_____ Other: ____

• There are several reasons why you may have had a hard time with the previous question. Perhaps you never learned to share your feelings. Maybe you've never been allowed to really be aware of your feelings. Perhaps you've been taught that feelings are bad. Or maybe you're so overwhelmed by a barrage of feelings that you can't distinguish one from another.

FREEDOM: Feelings simply are.
Feelings are natural and normal.
I am responsible for what I do with my feelings, but I am not responsible for having them.

Actions

Hear the words of Paul: "For what I am doing, I do not understand. For what I will to do, that I do not practice; but what I hate, that I do" (Romans 7:15 NKJV).

- Have you ever felt the frustration he expresses?

    ____ Yes, often.
    ____ Yes, from time to time.
    ____ Rarely.
    ____ No, not at all.

- Most of us can identify with what Paul says. We act the way we don't want to act. We also *react* in ways we don't want to. Reacting gives another person undeserved and unhealthful control over us. Again a choice is involved—and the choice is yours. Can you repeat the following pledge to yourself? You may find that you have to repeat it frequently—and that's okay!

    I choose not to let my ex-spouse push my buttons.
    I will act rather than react.

FREEDOM: I can choose to act, not react.

Reaping

- As I think back over the week, I realize that I took responsibility when I:

- This week I will assume responsibility for my present situation by:

- This week, instead of shooting for nothing, I will assume responsibility for my future by—

    ___ clarifying my goals.
    ___ talking to a person who can help me reach a goal (be specific about which goal and which person!).
    ___ spending time alone to get to know my hopes and dreams.
    ___ spending time with God in prayer and study—I want my goals to be His goals for me.
    ___ other: _____.

- This week I will carry the following verse or statement of freedom with me to replace any negative thoughts that come to mind:

- This week I will allow myself to *feel* my feelings. I may even risk sharing them with a friend. _____ would be a good listener I could trust.

- This week I will strive to act in a situation rather than react to it. I will count to ten, for instance, before responding to something my ex-spouse says.

FREEDOM: Assuming responsibility is not easy.
Assuming responsibility takes time.
But assuming responsibility is an important part of my own growth—and God will help me through it.

P.S.

Chapter 5

Assuming Responsibility For My Children

Sowing

"Be kind to each other, tenderhearted, forgiving one another, just as God has forgiven you because you belong to Christ" (Ephesians 4:32 TLB).

- Why should we believers be kind, tenderhearted, and forgiving in our behavior toward one another?

Paul always spoke about the practical things in the Christian life. He did not live in the clouds of biblical doctrine all the time, as some would have us believe. Much of his writing to the early Church was highly relational. He wanted the members of God's family to learn how to live with each other in peace and harmony.

The early Christians were just like today's models. They had to be reminded and encouraged repeatedly. Paul did this by constantly reminding them what Christ had done for them. They were "forgiven" and they "belonged." It was this spirit that they were to show to one another.

God's relational glue is comprised of kindness, tenderheartedness (a warm spirit), and forgiveness. God's love gives us these ingredients in great quantities. We are to transmit them to our brothers and sisters in God's family (*Every Single Day,* pp. 69-70).

- What is one act of kindness that you have done during the past week?

- How can a warm spirit (tenderheartedness) help you live according to Jesus Christ's greatest commandment—to "love the Lord your God with all your heart... and love your neighbor as yourself"?

- How does forgiveness lead to harmony between people?

Kindness, tenderheartedness, and forgiveness help members of God's family live together in peace and harmony. They also help members of your nuclear family live together in peace and harmony because they help you deal with your children during this time of pain and adjustment as you strive to fulfill your God-given responsibility toward them. This lesson will offer you insights and practical suggestions about how to be a parent to your children. Let this lesson also encourage you not to let your children be orphans of your divorce. As I said in the tapes and as I can't emphasize enough, parents don't divorce their kids when they divorce each other.

Tending

FREEDOM: Raising children as a single parent is not impossible.

- Which problem common to single parents is most pressing for you right now? If you seem to be surrounded by all four, rank them from greatest (1) to least (4). Read through the points which follow the list.

    ____ "My circuits are on overload."
    ____ "Where are you when I need you?"
    ____ "I don't get any respect."
    ____ "Help! I'm a prisoner!"

"My circuits are on overload." Be honest with yourself, with God, with trusted friends, and with people who are in a similar situation. Pent-up frustrations won't stay inside forever, and when they

come out they're likely to be directed toward the children you are trying so hard to love.

"Where are you when I need you?" An amicable relationship with the children's other parent will help the two of you be an effective mother and father. Remember this fact when you are tempted to let communication with your ex-spouse die.

"I don't get any respect." Receiving respect often comes in return for respect that is offered. Are you respectful of your former mate when you speak about him/her in front of the children? Do you respect your children as they deal with their pain and sense of loss in their own way?

"Help! I'm a prisoner!" All of us need to work on keeping our lives in balance. The "how-to's" can be difficult, and they vary from situation to situation. Again, let trusted friends help you gain a more objective perspective of your life.

FREEDOM: I am not the only person ever to struggle with being a single parent—and this struggle is appropriate because the task is difficult!

The following guidelines are designed to help you be an effective single mother or single father. Look closely at each one of them. Applying them to your life will restore some of the joys and rewards of parenting.

1. Don't try to be both parents to your children.

• How have you been trying to be both mother and father to your children?

• How do you feel in this unnatural and impossible role you've defined for yourself?

• Have you tried explaining to your children that you can't be both mother and father to them, but that you will work hard at being the best mother/father you can be? Good communication is as important in a parent-child relationship as it is in any other relationship.

2. Don't force your children into playing the role of the departed parent.

• Have you asked, either verbally or implicitly, your son to be a daddy or your daughter to be a mommy?

• Think about how you feel under the self-imposed pressure to be both mother and father. What similar feelings might your son feel about being forced to be a daddy or your daughter to be a mommy?

• A child needs to be a child! Don't hesitate to give your children new jobs or responsibilities around the house, but don't force them to take on an adult or parental role.

3. Be the parent you are.

• Why is it tempting to be a buddy or pal instead of Mom/Dad?

• Again, put yourself in your child's place. Does he/she need you to be a buddy? Or does he/she need you to continue to be a parent, thereby providing stability and continuity during the turmoil of a divorce?

• A parent—*you*—needs to be the parent! Don't abdicate that role. Don't escape into a childlike role. That will help no one!

4. Be honest with your children.

• How truthful have you been?

    ____ I've done the best I could.
    ____ I didn't want to hurt them so I fudged a little.
    ____ I told them as much as I thought they could handle.

____ I was honest—and it was worth the pain we all felt, the pain that now we all share.
____ Other: _____.

• How can your honesty be an important gift to your children? See Richard Gardner's perspective on page 62 of the text.

5. Don't put down your ex-spouse in front of your children.

• Why is it very tempting and quite easy to say negative things about your ex-spouse?

• What would be accomplished by such talk?

• Let me repeat something from the text: "Most children don't really care who did what to whom. What they care about is what is going to happen to them" (p. 62). Concentrate your energy on reassuring and loving your children rather than on bad-mouthing your ex-spouse!

6. Don't make your children undercover agents who report on the other parent's current activities.

• How could playing the role of spy for you affect your children's feelings about you?

• Why is it unfair to put a child in the middle between his/her divorcing parents?

• At times it's hard to be an adult, but this time is a *must*. Don't force your children to play "I Spy" for you.

7. The children of divorce need both a mother and a father.

- Do you have the right to deprive your children of their other parent? Only occasionally—as in an instance of molestation or physical, emotional, and psychological abuse—will the answer be yes.

- How would you feel if your former spouse decided that your children didn't need you?

- Parents are forever. This implies the necessity of a continuing relationship between your children and their other parent *and* between you and him/her.

8. Don't become a "Disneyland Daddy" or a "Magic Mountain Mommy."

- Why is this an easy trap to fall into?

- List three activities which you can enjoy with your child around your house or apartment. I'll get your brainstorming session started!

> Read a book together.
> Make homemade ice cream.
> Walk to the park.
> Write a letter to a grandparent.
> _____
> _____
> _____

- Use your imagination! Better yet, use your children's imaginations. Ask them what they would like to do—and then do it together!

9. Share your dating life and social interests with your child.

- Is this a good idea? Why or why not?

- Have you been honest with your children? Write down their responses to your behavior.

- Be honest with your children, yet let them still be children. They are not spies, "Dear Abby's," or counselors. Neither are they the enemy which should be kept in the dark at all costs.

10. Help your children keep the good memories of your past marriage alive.

- Will this project be healthy for your child? Why or why not?

- How can this project be healthy for you?

- Taking away your children's good memories is robbery. It is also an invitation to future bitterness, distrust, and cynicism about marriage. You can choose to keep them free of this unhealthy baggage as they grow.

11. Work out a management-and-existence statement for your children with your ex-spouse.

- How would this help you in your role as a single parent?

- How would your children benefit?

- The possible benefits seem to far outweigh the negatives involved in the development of this agreement. I would encourage you to take this step for your children's sake as well as for your own.

12. If possible, try not to disrupt the many areas in your children's lives that offer them safety and security.

- List some of the different people, activities, or involvements which offer your children a sense of security.

- If moving away from this support system is—or has been—necessary, which elements can you work together to find at your new home?

- The key concept here is adventure! Changes can be threatening—or they can be exciting doors to new experiences. Choose to help your children regard change as adventure.

13. If your child does not resume normal development and growth in his/her life within a year of the divorce, he/she may need the special care and help of a professional counselor.

- Who can help you watch your children and note the ways they are handling the divorce? Don't hesitate to enlist neighbors, the mothers of your child's friends, and schoolteachers in this task!

- Be prepared. Find out the names of two or three reputable counselors. Talk to people they have worked with and then meet with the counselor yourself.

   1)

   2)

   3)

- We take our children to the dentist for their cavities and to the doctor for the flu. We can likewise take them to counselors or psychologists for any emotional healing they need.

FREEDOM: Being a single parent is a skill to be learned—and I will learn it!

Assuming Responsibility for My Children • 45

Reaping

In reading through the 13 guidelines, you may have noticed some recurring themes:

- Being a single parent doesn't change a parent's call to be unselfish. If anything, that call is only intensified.

- Being a single parent also involves—
    - the call to honesty when you yourself may be a victim of dishonesty.
    - the call to be fair when your own situation is anything but fair.
    - the call to maintain a working relationship with your ex-spouse, whatever has happened and however he/she is acting now.
    - the call to be strong in your role as mother/father despite the temptation to throw your hands up in frustration or despair.
    - the call to let your children be children in the midst of the very adult problem of divorce.

- Set some goals for yourself as you accept the challenge and rise to the adventure of this changed parental status:

    —I will become a better father/mother by:

    —I will strive to be honest with my children about what is happening. I will begin by clarifying the details about:

    —Having looked back on the ideas of Guideline 8, this week I will do the following activity with my children:

    —This week I will work on keeping my children's good memories of my marriage alive by—

1. not making negative remarks about their father/mother.
2. reminding them of the fun we had when we _____.
3. other: _____.

Yes, being a single parent is difficult, but it can be done. And it can be a rewarding and fulfilling experience for you as well as for your children.

FREEDOM: A child can grow through divorce too.

P.S.

Chapter 6

Assuming Responsibility For My Future

Sowing

"What a God he is! How perfect in every way! All his promises prove true. He is a shield for everyone who hides behind him. For who is God except our Lord? Who but he is as a rock?" (Psalm 18:30 TLB).

• List the aspects of God's character which the psalmist sings about in this verse.

Have you ever run out of superlatives when describing your best friend to someone? You want that person to know how you feel about your friend and what he means to you. David felt that way about God. Although he had his struggles with God, he still affirmed Him to others.

David tells us in this verse that God is five different things. As we look at them, ask yourself if you could describe God to your friends in these terms.

First, God is perfect in every way. That is difficult for us to grasp because our world is filled with imperfections.

Second, we are told that God stands behind His promises: They are true. When God says something, He does it.

Third, God provides a shield for us to hide behind. When the world throws its heavy artillery at us, we need to shield ourselves while we regroup. God provides a secure hiding place for us when we need it.

Fourth, He is our Lord. That's personal, not general. We belong to Him and He belongs to us.

Finally, He is a rock. For me, that represents stability. He doesn't change game plans and agenda from day to day. He is solid and He is there for me—today and tomorrow! (*Every Single Day*, pp. 201-02).

- Which of these five truths about God do you have the hardest time believing?

- Has God ever given you reason to doubt the perfection of His ways, His faithfulness to His promises, His personal lordship of your life, or the stability of His plans for you? Don't attribute the behavior and free choices of imperfect and sinful people to the all-loving God! But *do* talk to God about where your faith in Him may be weak right now. Call on Him to help your unbelief (Mark 9:24).

- Which of the five truths about God offers you hope for the future?

As this lesson will emphasize, each of us needs to assume responsibility for the future, but that doesn't mean going it alone. We need to make decisions and take steps, but we can and should do this with the guidance of our perfect, steadfast, protective, personal, and stable God. Claim the truth of this personality profile and step into the future—step into tomorrow—with confidence and eager anticipation of what it holds for you. God *will* be with you!

Tending

FREEDOM: It's normal for me to feel unenthusiastic, skeptical, or hopeless about the future.

- Whether or not you completed the exercise on pages 70-71 of the text, take the time now to list ten things you are looking forward to in the next several days and weeks. Let your imagination go free. Are you looking forward to a friend's birthday celebra-

Assuming Responsibility for My Future • 49

tion? A long-awaited letter? Learning something new at work? Experimenting with your wok? Taking the risk of making a new friend?

1)

2)

3)

4)

5)

6)

7)

8)

9)

10)

• If you had a difficult time listing ten things, learn something about yourself from that fact.

I learned that:

• You might also learn something about yourself from this observation:

> I've noticed three kinds of people—those who watch things happen, those who make things happen, and those who don't know what's happening.

If you have goals for yourself, you are probably a person who makes things happen. If you aren't sure this description fits you right now, you can work toward that goal—but your cocoon will have to go! You will be letting go of that cocoon when you make plans for the future and then follow them.

FREEDOM: I am free to fail.

We are all human. We all therefore make mistakes and all experience failure. The healthy way to deal with this inevitable failure is to learn something from the experience and then move forward. Such movement can sometimes be difficult, and then it's both wise and helpful to consult with a trusted friend or respected counselor. These people can help us set realistic goals for ourselves. The following five guidelines are also helpful.

1. Evaluate your present situation.

- Evaluate your current financial situation. Establish a workable budget.

    What are your monthly expenses?

    What is your monthly income?

    Can some expenses be reduced, if not completely eliminated?

    What options do you have for increasing your income?

    Will the steps toward an increased income call for any extra expenses, whether temporary or ongoing?

- Look at your job situation.

    Are you working now?

    If so, are you satisfied?

    If so, what are you working toward in your job?

    If you aren't employed, where can you go for assistance?

    If you aren't employed, what can you do to rebuild your sense of self-confidence and self-esteem? Try the Bible! Also try low-pressure projects which will give you the feeling of having accomplished something.

- Consider your career path.

This is the same question you've been asked all your life: "What do you want to be when you grow up?" Let the sky be the limit as you answer the question. If nothing were impossible, where would you like to be in five years? In ten years?

- This three-part evaluation is the starting point for making plans. The following verse is added incentive.

FREEDOM: "I will instruct you and teach you in the way you should go; I will guide you with My eye" (Psalm 32:8 NKJV).

2. Explore new and potential situations.

- How do you feel about the future? About changes? About the new and the unknown?

- You don't need to be bullied by feelings of fear, a lack of hope, or a sense of discouragement. Instead, choose to see the future as an adventure. You can choose also to see this adventure as being held in the hands of a loving God.

FREEDOM: I choose to be an explorer and adventurer in my approach to the future.

I choose to follow God along this path. (See Psalm 119:105 and Jeremiah 29:11.)

3. Establish short-term and long-term goals.

- Why is it important to establish long-term goals?

- Why is it important and helpful to establish short-term goals as well? How can they serve as stepping-stones toward your long-range plans?

4. Don't be afraid of commitments.

- Are you afraid of commitments right now?

Yes, terrified!   No, not at all.

- Some fear of commitment—some hesitation to be vulnerable—is understandable and quite appropriate for someone experiencing a divorce. Let me remind you, though, that one broken commitment doesn't mean that every future commitment will be broken. A past failure doesn't mean only failure in the future, especially when we take the time to learn from the past. Think carefully about the following things and respond as specifically as you can.

Since your divorce, what have you learned about—

- your feelings?

- your ability to deal with new situations?

- the way you cope with pain?

- friendship?

- forgiveness?

- the role of communication in a relationship?

- the importance of honesty?

- your expectations for a marriage relationship?

- your standards for yourself?

- God?

- Read through the Ten Commandments (pp. 77-78) for other insights about the past, ways to cope with the present, and ideas to carry you into the future. Rewrite each commandment in your own words so that it speaks specifically to your current situation.

5. Trust God with your future.

• What does the phrase "Trust God" mean to you as it is used in this context? (I offer my own perspective on page 78 of the text.)

• How can trusting God be active rather than passive? In other words, how is trusting God different from merely waiting for Him to act?

FREEDOM: Trust in the Lord with all your heart,
And lean not on your own understanding;
In all your ways acknowledge Him,
And He shall direct your paths (Proverbs 3:5,6 NKJV).

Reaping

• This week I will take a risk. Knowing that it is okay to fail, I will risk:

• I will seek to improve my present job situation by—

____ outlining the progress I've made since coming to work and determining the prospects for the future.
____ gathering information about the company's organizational structure, its advancement policies, and its history of promotions.
____ talking to the boss about advancement possibilities.
____ investigating similar opportunities with different companies.
____ other: _____.

• I will consider the career path I'm on and alternatives which might be better in the long run. I will—

    ____ brainstorm with a friend about possible options.
    ____ set aside 30 minutes for daydreaming: "If I could do/be anything, I would _____."
    ____ visit a local college's career planning center and familiarize myself with that resource.
    ____ talk to_____,a person who holds a position I only fantasize about right now.
    ____ other: _____.

• Choose one or two long-term goals from the beginning of the "Tending" section. Below, define two or three short-term goals which can help you achieve the grander ones—and then begin to tackle a few of those short-term goals this week.

LONG-TERM GOAL NUMBER ONE:

Short-term goals:

a)

b)

c)

LONG-TERM GOAL NUMBER TWO:

Short-term goals:

a)

b)

c)

• I will work on improving my level of trust in God by getting to know Him better. To do this, I will—

    ____ attend a worship service.
    ____ spend five minutes a day reading the Bible.
    ____ start each day with two or three minutes of prayer.
    ____ close each day with a prayer of thanksgiving for what happened that day.

___ set aside ten minutes to be quiet with God.
___ pray with a friend.
___ other: _____.

P.S.

Chapter 7

Finding a Family

Sowing

"He has given you Paul and Apollos and Peter as your helpers. He has given you the whole world to use, and life and even death are your servants" (1 Corinthians 3:22 TLB).

- Who has God given you—either someone in the past or someone involved in your life right now—as your "helper"?

How would you like to have Paul, Apollos, and Peter as your personal friends and helpers? They certainly were a dynamic trio. With friends like that, you would be a lot stronger in the faith and more courageous in your walk.

Somehow, the Corinthian believers did not realize the value of this trio. They probably did just what you and I do with our good friends—take them for granted. We seldom realize how important friends are to us until they move to another town.

Whom has God given you as friends and helpers in your life? The good friends we have are not there by accident. I believe that God has a way of bringing people into our lives to support us and care for us. Sometimes we move through life so fast that we don't allow people time to connect to us and become God's blessing in our lives....

Are you open to God's bringing new friends and helpers into your life today? The next person you meet may be by divine direction. Keep your heart open. He may need you just as much as you need him! (*Every Single Day*, p. 222).

- Write down the names of two or three friends who have helped you be strong in your faith and more courageous in the face of life's hurdles. Be specific about what you appreciate about each of these people.

- Have you taken such good friends for granted? Thank God right now for bringing them into your life. I also encourage you to pick up the phone or a piece of paper and a pen. Let these people know that you appreciate them!

- Having thought about the way God has already blessed you with friends, consider how open you are right now about meeting other people He wants to bring into your life.

    ____ I am open to the blessings of new friends which God wants to give me.
    ____ I want friends and helpers, but right now I'm nervous about taking the risk of getting to know someone.
    ____ I want new friends, but the risk of being vulnerable and possibly being hurt outweighs any benefits that might come with finding a new friend.
    ____ I'm not ready to risk getting close to another person.

- Whatever your answer above, read again the last three sentences of this lesson's devotional. Have you thought of someone needing you as much as—if not more than—you need him/her?

Developing a friendship can be risky business. I have found my church involvement to be a safe place for taking this kind of risk. I have found support and encouragement in God's family—the family we will look at closely in this lesson.

Tending

- First, consider the family you were born into.

    —How did your family receive you?

    —How did you receive them?

—What did they do for you?

—What did you do for them?

• Now how is this family reacting to you and your divorce?

• If you are disappointed or hurt by their reactions, try to understand that they may not understand the pain you feel, how to help, or what to say, and that they aren't responsible for the divorce or their own mixed emotions. And if you feel alone right now because of their inability to help, claim this promise:

FREEDOM: God is our refuge and strength,
A very present help in trouble (Psalm 46:1 NKJV).

• Look for a moment at the family that you married into.

—What dreams did you have (or do you still have) for this family?

—Do you still feel a part of this family?

—How are these people reacting to you and your divorce?

• If you are disappointed or hurt by their reaction, again try to understand that they are struggling with their own confusion, hurt, shock, disappointment, and loyalty to their own son or daughter.

• If you are feeling estranged from your natural family and from your former spouse's family, let me encourage you to discover or rediscover the family of God. When we, God's children, bear one another's burdens, we fulfill the law which our heavenly Father has given us and we build a family which reflects the tender love and constant support which God offers each one of us (see Galatians 6:2). Consider these facts about God's family.

—God's family is a "forever family."
—You join God's family by receiving His Son, Jesus Christ,

and recognizing Him as the new Director of your life.
— Membership in this family means growth every day, and that growth comes from study, worship, prayer, and talking with other family members.
— The family of God—huge and enduring as it is—provides its members a sense of belonging that nothing else can.
— Members of God's family have responsibilities to each other as we help each other live according to Jesus' instructions. (See page 89 of the text.)
— We can't lose our membership in the family of God: "All that the Father gives Me will come to Me, and the one who comes to Me I will by no means cast out" (John 6:37 NKJV).

• What is most appealing about this description of God's "forever family"? In other words, what would you most like to find in this family?

• Write out the following instructions for living in God's family. At the end you'll have a description of the kind of community that God wants us to share with each other.

—Ephesians 4:1-3

—1 Corinthians 10:24

—Hebrews 12:14,15

—1 Thessalonians 5:14,15

Reaping

• What will improve your relationship with members of your family? Check whatever answers are appropriate.

____ Your forgiveness of them
____ Their forgiveness of you
____ Time
____ Patience
____ Prayer
____ Swallowing your pride

___ Dropping your defensive stance
___ Open, honest, and sensitive communication
___ God's healing power
___ Other: _____

- Turn one of your choices into a goal.

    This week I will take a step toward improving my relationship with my family by _____
    _____.

- What might improve your relationship with your ex-spouse's family? Consider some of the elements on the previous list.

- Take time to consider whether pursuing a relationship with your former in-laws is a wise or worthwhile move at this time. If after careful thought and prayer you feel that it is, set yourself a goal for taking a positive step this week. If you don't believe that it is wise to take such a step now, set yourself the goal of praying regularly about the hurt on both sides of the break.

- What local part of God's family would you like to become more involved with? List three or four possibilities here.

- Now set yourself a goal:

    This week I will call about (which group?) _____
    and find out about it. I will ask if any members come from my neighborhood, and if so I will contact him/her about going to the meeting together.

- If becoming involved in God's family means that you first need to become His son or daughter, pray this simple prayer:

    God, thank You for the invitation to be part of Your family. Thank You for sending Your son, Jesus Christ, to die for my sins so that I can become Your son/daughter. Teach me to trust You with my life. Help me to love people more. Train me to follow You more closely. In Your Son's name. Amen.

FREEDOM: Behold what manner of love the Father has bestowed on us, that we should be called children of God! (1 John 3:1 NKJV).

P.S.

Chapter 8

Finding and Experiencing Forgiveness

Sowing

"If we confess our sins, He is faithful and righteous to forgive us our sins and to cleanse us from all unrighteousness (1 John 1:9 NASB).

• What does this verse teach about the kind of God our heavenly Father is?

> Have you ever struggled with admitting you were wrong in a certain situation or discussion? Remember how hard it was? Wouldn't it be great to always be right and never have to confess that you were wrong?
>
> God created us to be very human. Along with our humanness comes the conflict of right and wrong. God seemed to know that we would make mistakes, so He provided a way to help us take care of them. His formula is, Confession equals cleansing and forgiveness. It's not an easy formula to live with, but it is the only one that helps us keep a right relationship with both God and man.
>
> Perhaps you have noticed that this promise begins with an *if*. That might prompt you to ask what happens if we don't confess wrongs or sins. From my experience, lack of confession leads to the guilt trap, the anger syndrome, and the pits of depression.
>
> Many of us cart around things that need to be confessed to God. Only when we confess them, admit them, and own

up to them can God do anything with them. His promise becomes a cleansing therapy that will keep us whole (*Every Single Day*, pp. 47-48).

- Why isn't forgiveness "an easy formula" for you to live with?

- Have you experienced the guilt, anger, and/or depression which come when we don't confess our sin? Which of these three feelings do you struggle with most?

- What feelings have you experienced when you've talked to God about a time you were wrong, a mistake you made, an incident when you hurt someone, or your failure to walk closely with Him?

In this lesson we'll deal with the issue of forgiveness as it pertains to your divorce. Whatever the details of your particular situation (you may feel like the innocent victim or you may realize the pain you have caused others) you must come to a point of forgiveness, and that will involve forgiving yourself and forgiving others as well as accepting God's forgiveness.

Tending

Seeds of forgiveness can be cultivated in five areas of your life, and we will look at each one of them.

1. God forgives me!

- For what attitudes and actions—especially surrounding your divorce—do you need to receive God's forgiveness? Be honest with yourself and with God. Let go of the unnecessary baggage of guilt and self-hatred. You can do this only when you acknowledge your failure to live up to God's ideal for marriage and when you recognize the other errors which surrounded your divorce.

Finding and Experiencing Forgiveness • 65

- Read again the simple prayer on pages 98 and 99 of your text. This short talk with God can mark a new beginning in your life.

- Read John 8:3-11. Write verse 11 below, and personalize it. Include your name. Hear Jesus speaking those words to you.

FREEDOM: (Write the verse which opened this lesson, and write it so that it speaks directly to you.)

_____

_____

2. I forgive me!

- Which is harder for you—accepting God's forgiveness or forgiving yourself?

- For what actions or attitudes are you struggling to forgive yourself? Be as specific as possible. This will help you let go of the burden of guilt and the habit of self-flagellation.

- Review the definitions of forgiving yourself that I list on pages 99 and 100 of the text. List below those statements which are, for you, a declaration of independence.

FREEDOM: _____

_____

_____

- Consider also this statement of freedom from God's Word:

FREEDOM: But God demonstrates His own love toward us, in that while we were still sinners, Christ died for us (Romans 5:8 NKJV).

- Remember this verse when you are less forgiving of yourself than your loving God is!

3. I forgive my ex-spouse.

- Forgiving your ex-spouse will take time. It will also take a conscious decision on your part as you choose to forgive him or her. When you forgive your ex-spouse, however, you are actually freeing yourself from a burden of hatred and resentment. You are freeing yourself from thoughts about that person which would continue to control your emotions if not your actions as well. Forgiveness, though, does not need to involve the potentially condescending pronouncement to the other party, "I forgive you."

- Consider Jesus' instructions about forgiveness and Paul's echo of this teaching. Write the following verses below:

    —Matthew 6:14,15

    —Colossians 3:13

    —Ephesians 4:32

- Spend some time talking to God about your struggle to forgive your ex-spouse.

4. My ex-spouse forgives me.

- Receiving the forgiveness of your ex-spouse may mean asking for that forgiveness. Such asking must be done without a condescending, "holier-than-thou" attitude.

    —Examine your motives.
    —Ask God to guide you as to what to say and when to talk to your former mate.
    —Understand that asking for forgiveness involves admitting your weaknesses and your contributions to the divorce.

- Which of the following responses do you expect?

    ____ Gracious acceptance of your request and a statement of forgiveness.
    ____ Laughter.

____ Hostile rejection.
____ Being ignored.
____ No response at all.
____ Other: _____.

• Anticipating the possible response may help you deal with the real-life situation. Consider, though, whether the response of your former mate really has any bearing on your request for forgiveness. Would his/her rejection of you when you ask for forgiveness invalidate your act of repentance? The answer, in case there is any doubt, is *no!* When you acknowledge your responsibility for your divorce and when you approach your ex-spouse, you have fulfilled your responsibility. You are free to go forward from here.

5. I will forgive and forget.

• Forgetting comes with time. As God heals you, forgetting will be part of the process. And, as I alluded to earlier, forgiveness takes time. It is an ongoing process which the God who forgave you will help you through.

• Reread the poem "Prayer for the Divorced" on page 103. Which line(s) touched you? What message does the poem have for you?

Reaping

• In which of the five areas of your life would you like to experience forgiveness?

• Set goals for yourself in each of the five areas. If you have already experienced forgiveness, thank God for that!

—God's forgiveness

—Forgiveness of yourself

—Forgiving your ex-spouse

—Receiving forgiveness from your ex-spouse

—Forgetting

FREEDOM: As far as the east is from the west,
So far has He removed our transgressions from us (Psalm 103:12 NKJV).

P.S.

Chapter 9

Thirty-Seven
Going on Seventeen

Sowing

"There is no fear in love; but perfect love casts out fear, because fear involves punishment, and the one who fears is not perfected in love" (1 John 4:18 NASB).

• When has your love for someone cast out the fear that he or she was feeling about something? Think of young children, for instance, or a friend who was facing a hurdle you had once cleared in your own life. Jot down a few details about that situation.

Have you ever made a list of all your fears? It could run all the way from your fear of getting a speeding ticket to cracking your dentures on peanut brittle. The problem with fears is that they seldom become realities. They are ghosts that hide in the closets of our minds, and only come out when we aren't looking. John was aware that even Christians have fears. He knew that fear could prevent the people of God from living a fulfilled life. He knew that only one thing could eliminate fear from the life of the Christian. That one thing was knowing that God's love was stronger in a believer's life than all the fears he could conjure up.

Have you ever tried to give your fears a dose of love? A common fear is the fear of what will happen tomorrow. How do you deal with that fear?

The Scripture tells me that God is in charge of tomorrow.

If I believe that He loves me enough to take me through tomorrow, then there is nothing about it I need to fear. His love will penetrate that fear and remove it from my life (*Every Single Day*, p. 237).

• What fears are haunting you right now? Don't dwell on this question, but do list three or four things that readily come to mind.

• In his Gospel, John teaches about the love of God:

For God so loved the world that He gave His only begotten Son, that whoever believes in Him should not perish but have everlasting life (John 3:16 NKJV).

What bearing does this fact have on the fears you just listed?

• Look up these other words about God's love for you and me. Let their truth replace the fears of your life.

—Romans 5:8

—1 John 4:7-9

—Romans 8:38,39

Perhaps a fear you listed was fear of the future. One aspect of that perfectly understandable feeling may be your nervousness about once again entering the dating scene. This lesson will focus on the challenging and frustrating, yet potentially quite rewarding, adventure of dating again.

Tending

• In the text I claim that it is a mistake to jump into any kind of relationship until you have had time to adjust to your divorce and to the new demands it has placed on you. Do you agree? Why or why not? As you consider my claim, jot down some of the pros and cons of giving yourself time to heal and adjust.

- Read through the list of fears which are common to people coming out of a divorce. Indicate with a checkmark your greatest fear.

    ____ Can I be sure that the relationship will last this time?
    ____ Can I ever trust another man/woman again?
    ____ Will I make the same mistakes again?
    ____ Can I be happy if I marry again?
    ____ What if I don't find someone?
    ____ Will I feel confident and sure enough to begin dating?
    ____ Other (or a combination of two or more listed): _____

FREEDOM: Healing takes time.
Learning to trust takes time.
My time line is unique to me.

- The questions above point out a choice you can make between the risk of reaching out and the risk of regret. You may reach out and be hurt again, or you may choose never again to be vulnerable and thereby sentence yourself to an isolated existence which will very likely take you to a point of emptiness and regret for opportunities not taken and friendships missed. If you do reach out and if you are hurt, you will survive. God will be with you. Your church family and close friends will stand by you. What choice—whether consciously or by default—are you making right now?

FREEDOM: I choose to _____.

- The fears we just looked at are not helpful if they immobilize us. They are helpful, though, when they caution us to think about the step we're taking into a relationship. Answer these questions for yourself.

What have I learned about myself through my divorce? A corollary question is, Have I taken enough time to learn about my strengths and weaknesses, my typical behaviors in a relationship, or my ability to communicate?

Has enough time elapsed to let the dust settle?

_____ Yes _____ No _____ I'm not sure

There is no magic length of time for every person. Healing happens in different ways for each of us. Be sensitive to how much you've healed. Be patient with yourself. You'll then be able to enter a new friendship as a stronger person.

Am I building healthy relationships? Begin to answer this question by first considering with whom you are building relationships right now. Are they people who are growing? Or are they too close to their own divorce and pain? Is there a balance between giving and receiving in these relationships? What are you giving? What are you receiving?

How much of my past marriage am I dragging into my new relationship? We are all products of our own experiences; that fact cannot be changed. Still, we need not carry excess baggage with us as we journey through life. Are you still talking about your marriage? Is it hard for you to leave behind that part of your past? If so, you may want to give yourself a little more time before you enter a new relationship.

• Having dealt with your fears and carefully thought about the four points of caution, consider now the issue of trust.

With my trust in God and with His help, I can begin again.

• Do you trust God? Write your own freedom statement. Choose a verse from the Bible or an idea from my discussion of this topic on page 111 of the text.

FREEDOM: With the help of God, I can learn to love and trust in new ways.

_____

_____

• How can God be a part of your learning process?

• How can a good friend *of the same sex* help you learn to trust?

I will trust that God is doing a new work in my life and will continue to do it. If and when I remarry, it will be the richest experience of my life.

• Is it easier for you to trust God or other people? Why?

• How can trust in God help you trust other people?

• Write your own statement of trust. How easy is it for you to trust God right now? Be honest with yourself and with Him!

• Write Romans 8:28 below and let that verse help you trust God more.

FREEDOM: _____

_____

Reaping

- Which fear would you like to put to rest in the next several weeks?

- Develop a goal that will help you do this. The goal can involve choosing again and again not to let the fear control you. The goal can involve taking a small risk of sharing your ideas, feelings, or dreams. The goal can involve turning to God for His healing, His guidance, and His support.

   This week I will _____

   _____

   _____.

- Which caution spoke directly to you and your current situation?

- Write out a caution to carry with you this week. The caution may be a prayer or a reminder of a lesson you've learned the hard way.

- In which current relationship can you risk sharing a little more of yourself? This will be a step of learning to trust more—and you have a lot to gain by taking that step!

   Before adding your P.S., spend some time jotting down your ideas about the following excerpt from the text: Describe the person you married the first time and the kind of person you would like to marry in the future. This valuable exercise will help you understand your fears, follow words of caution, and sow seeds of the ability to trust.

P.S.

Chapter 10

Remarriage—Yours, Mine, And Maybe Our Families'

Sowing

"My God shall supply all your needs according to His riches in glory in Christ Jesus" (Philippians 4:19 NASB).

- What are some of your daily needs?

Have you ever planned and plotted to get some desired item? You just knew you couldn't live without it. Then, after you acquired it, it sat around and you hardly ever used it. That's why we have so many garage sales in our country. We have garages full of things we had to have but seldom use.

There is a vast difference between what we want and what we need in life. Our want list is usually taken from the merchandisers who really want our money for their products. Our need list is more geared to what we really need to keep alive and well.

On the nonmaterial side, we need love, affirmation, friendship, meaning and purpose in our lives. And that's just a small part of the list of intangibles.

Paul tells us that God promises to meet each of us on the "need" level of our lives. God's riches are so vast that He can just tap into His inexhaustible supply and distribute them freely to us.

Have you been moping recently over the things you don't have instead of thanking God for what you do have? God always knows what will be good for us, and those are the things He sends our way. God is in the business of meeting our needs—even the most gigantic ones. Trust Him today for yours! (*Every Single Day*, p. 47).

- Look again at your list above. Did some "wants" creep into your "needs" list? Cross those off.

- Having read today's devotional, do you want to add any items to your list?

- Circle those items which God is providing for you right now.

- Let me ask you again the question I posed in the text devotional: "Have you been moping recently over the things you don't have instead of thanking God for what you do have?"

Trust God to meet your needs. Trust Him to know *what* is good for you and *when* it is good for you to receive it. Trust Him also to help you be a responsible steward of those things and people with which He does bless you. If, for instance, God seems to be leading you to remarriage with its joys and struggles, its new beginnings and new challenges, seek God's guidance and learn from this lesson.

Tending

(This tending should be done by both you and the person you may marry!)

- What feelings surface when you hear the word "remarriage"?

___ panic	___ fear	___ wariness
___ longing	___ caution	___ hostility
___ skepticism	___ enthusiasm	___ sense of wholeness
___ hope	___ impatience	___ other: _____

- Are you at peace with God about this decision to remarry? Honest introspection and sincere seeking after God's will are crucial steps in this decision-making process.

- The decision to marry must be made not only with your heart but also with your mind. Think through the following issues if you are considering remarriage. The nuts and bolts of everyday living call for careful thought rather than just warm feelings. Waiting until these situations occur will not help your new marriage start off strongly.

    —How many children are involved? Who will support them?

    —Where will they live?

    —Will some of your income have to go toward the support of an ex-spouse and children?

    —Where will you live? An old house has ghosts and memories which can haunt a new marriage.

    —How will the children address their new parents?

    —If your new mate is a noncustodial parent, where will his/her children stay when they visit you?

    —Will you be having to deal with legal adoptions and name changes for the children once you marry?

    —How will you and your new mate handle the discipline of each other's children?

Now that you're warmed up, think about the following six areas of possible conflict. They involve either an ongoing relationship with a former spouse, the fair treatment of children, or the finances of remarriage—three issues which will never seem to be totally resolved.

- To whom should you be loyal? First list your options. Then rank them, letting number 1 stand for the person who deserves the greatest loyalty from you.

- Now read through my discussion on pages 116 and 117 of the text. Do these hypothetical situations call into question the ranking you just did? Real life has a way of changing seemingly black-and-white issues into varying shades of gray!

- You may be wondering how you can win with stepchildren. What do you fear about the prospect of dealing with stepchildren?

- Imagine being one of the children. How would you want to be treated? In answering this question, you may provide yourself with some very effective guidelines for your role as a stepparent.

- How can you make stepchildren feel as important as your natural children? Brainstorm about this and the preceding question with your potential spouse.

FREEDOM: I am going to just be myself. Then I can work to become the best stepmother/stepfather I can be.

- What adjustments will you have to make in your lifestyle when the two families become one? To answer this, first describe the two different lifestyles. Will there be a significant difference between the weekdays and the weekends? Or does the new challenge involve blending your ways with your future spouse? How are the kids caught in the middle? What sacrifices are you being called to make as you adjust to your new situation? Again, jot down ideas, but then be sure to discuss these issues with your potential mate.

Remarriage • 81

- How are you to treat your spouse's ex-mate?

    —How much contact do you anticipate?

    —Are you able to be compassionate as you consider the ex-spouse's situation?

    —How amicable was the divorce settlement?

    —How might your new marriage help you deal with *your* ex-mate?

Again, think about these things and jot down ideas, but also plan to talk a lot with your future spouse about dealings with your ex-mates.

- How will you be related to new in-laws, former in-laws, and other friends? List the names of people who will be affected by your remarriage and note beside each name the reaction you have received or the reaction you expect.

- Another topic for thought and discussion is how you will deal with these relationships. For which ones will you fight? Which ones will be dissolved? How will you deal with the pain?

- How will you and your mate grow together in your marriage? Write down specific plans you have for making sure that you have time for each other, time to communicate, time to play together, time to work together, and time to worship God together.

Reaping

As with any growing thing, a remarriage does not take root immediately and bloom overnight. But careful and patient cultivation of the relationship will bring satisfaction and fulfillment that is well worth the wait. Such cultivation must be planned.

- This week my future mate and I will meet together

    (when?) _____

    (where?) _____

    to discuss—

    —children.

    —dealings with former spouse(s).

    —finances.

We will talk about our different lifestyles by comparing the profiles we sketched in the "Tending" section.

Date _____

Time _____

Place _____

- Plan for a time to talk about these issues as well:

    —What fears do you have about remarriage?

    —What role will God play in your life? In your mate's life? in your life together?

    —How important is communicating? How can you keep communication open and vital?

—Consider situations which could arise that would call into question your loyalty to each other. Talk them through carefully *now*, before the situation is a reality and emotions are at a fever pitch.

—How threatened is each of you by the other's ex-spouse? By the other's natural children?

• Define two goals for yourself that will help you prepare for your marriage. Consider those habits, attitudes, or behaviors which you would like to be free of, and plan a way to change and grow!

P.S.

Chapter 11

How I've Grown*

Sowing

"[Jesus] healed all who were sick. This was to fulfill what was spoken by the prophet Isaiah, 'He took our infirmities and bore our diseases' " (Matthew 8:16,17 RSV).

• Where have you seen God's healing touch in your own life or in the lives of people you know?

> Jesus really was in the healing business as He walked through the society of His time. He healed everyone who was sick, whether they came to Him as individuals or as groups. He healed people physically and emotionally. He never left anyone as He found them.
>
> Our lives are a collection of hurts and healings. Situations, people, and diseases bring many hurts into our lives. God wants to move through those hurts and bring His healing power to bear in us. God is still in the healing business today. He meets and heals physical needs. He heals the inner wounds that have scarred our emotions (*Every Single Day*, p. 36).

• Where do you need healing in your life?

• Have you talked to God specifically about that situation? If you

---

* Based on Chapters 11 and 12 in *Growing Through Divorce*.

have, keep it up! God calls us to be persistent in prayer. If you haven't prayed, do so now!

It's hard for us to realize our own growth or to recognize the healing that is happening in our lives. We are too close to the situation—we are living with the pain and the questions—to be able to see our progress. Often, however, we can look back and see clearly the moments and the friendships, the steps we took and the emotions we experienced, the hopelessness and the renewed hope—all part of the healing process. Wherever you are now on this path of healing—and you probably won't be able to say—you can gain some perspective of God's healing process as you read other people's stories.

Tending

Read through these personal accounts of healing in "How I've Grown Through My Divorce." These statements in Chapter 11 are written by people who have walked the very path that you are now walking.

- —Some ideas may be hard for you to believe.
- —Some experiences may seem too good to happen to you.
- —On some days, the words may seem like religious hype or Pollyanna optimism.
- —On some days, these people's words will hold out to you the hope and encouragement I intend them to have.

Highlight in your book (or better yet, jot down below) several ideas which—

- challenge you ("That sounds tough—but if he/she can do it, so can I!").
- encourage you ("I'm not the only one who's felt this way!").
- stand as goals for you ("I'd like to be able to say that someday!").
- teach you about God ("He really can forgive me! He really does love me!").

You may even want to include a few statements which you can't believe at all. You just may find yourself one day seeing the reality of those very things which right now you don't even believe can happen!

FREEDOM: I can't know what the future holds, but I can know the One who holds the future. Help me, God, to trust You and to walk with You into that future.

Reaping

Like Chapter 11, Chapter 12 in *Growing Through Divorce* focuses on people's personal experiences. If remarriage is too distant or too frightening or completely irrelevant for you right now, feel free to go on to the next chapter of this guide. However, if remarriage is something you are considering, read through this chapter and note those ideas which—

- alert you to the challenges that lie ahead.
- encourage you as you strive to build a strong, new marriage relationship.
- teach you about God's forgiveness as well as the important part He wants to have in your marriage.

Let me also exhort you once again to hold on to the painful lessons of your divorce. What mistakes can you avoid now? What new behaviors, ideas, attitudes, and priorities will make this new marriage strong?

P.S.

Chapter 12

Practical Pointers, How to Help, And One Last Word*

How to Keep the Scales of Justice from Tilting

Whether or not you want a divorce, get an attorney right away! Remember that a strong person asks for help—and all of us laypersons need help in understanding the tangle of laws surrounding a divorce. Protect yourself and your future by securing a competent attorney that you can trust. Pages 151-157 in *Growing Through Divorce* can help you choose an attorney and work with him or her effectively.

For most of you, this involvement in the legal world may be a new and rather frightening experience. If you've never spoken with an attorney, these feelings are appropriate. Acknowledge your fears (they'll be less powerful that way!) and then continue to work with a lawyer. There is too much at stake for you not to be working with an expert in legal issues. As someone has said, anyone experiencing a divorce needs three things—a good friend, a good attorney, and God—and, I might add, not necessarily in that order!

How to Help

Few if any of us ever clearly understand why we've had to go through certain painful times in our lives. Perhaps we will someday understand, but even now I can see how God uses people who have hurt in the past as wounded healers for people who are hurting now. After growing through your divorce, you will have some very valuable lessons to share with other people. This

---

* Based on Chapters 13-15 in *Growing Through Divorce*.

sharing does not mean just talking and lecturing. It also—and perhaps even more importantly—means knowing how to accept the person who is suffering. Right now, while you're still close to your own pain, make notes under each of these five headings about what your experience has taught you.

1. Don't judge. (How would you have wanted to be accepted and trusted?)

2. Listen with love and understanding. (How would you have wanted to be listened to? What did the best listeners in your life do?)

3. Be supportive in any way you can. (What were the most helpful ways in which people supported you? Or how would you have wanted people to support you?)

4. Give direction where you can. (What is the best way to offer your help? What characterized those people who were easiest for you to listen to as they offered their opinions and advice?)

5. Refer people to available resources. (Jot down several resources which you found helpful. Include information about job counseling, church and professional therapy, a competent lawyer, a good realtor, divorce recovery workshops, community college classes, and books.)

One Last Word

- What choice are you making day by day—if not on occasion moment by moment?

    ____   I am *going* through divorce.
    ____   I am *growing* through divorce.

- What freedoms are you carrying with you as you grow through your divorce? (I'm assuming that if you've made it to this point in the book, you have chosen to *grow through* rather than just *go through* your divorce!) Choose from your favorite Bible verses, from the Freedoms in this guide, and from the Ten Commandments listed on page 167 of the text.

FREEDOM: _____

_____

_____

FREEDOM: _____

_____

_____

FREEDOM: _____

_____

_____

I want to sow a few more seeds before you close this book.

Don't be anxious about tomorrow. God will take care of your tomorrow too. Live one day at a time (Matthew 6:34 TLB).

• What two or three things in your life immediately come to mind when you hear the word "worry"?

> Someone has said, "Today is the tomorrow you worried about yesterday." Most of us have that problem at least once a week. We tend to hurry through today as we build a mountain of worry about tomorrow. When that tomorrow comes, we just push all our worries a day ahead. Following this pattern, we could spend the rest of our lives worrying.
>
> Jesus knew that our human tendency would be to be anxious and worry about things, people, problems, events. Notice that His word about worry and being anxious is authoritative. He simply says not to do it. If that were all He said, it would be of little help, but He backs up His command with a promise. He says that He will take care of your

tomorrows and my tomorrows. That means living our lives in trust that tomorrow, as well as today, is really God's problem. He owns all our tomorrows. We don't.

Jesus offers us a command, a promise, and a solution as we live the days of our lives. The solution is found in centering on today—living it, embracing it, affirming it, enjoying it.

What's on your "tomorrow" agenda? Is it ruining your "today" as it tumbles through your mind? Give it to God and start living in today! (*Every Single Day*, pp. 16-17).

As you start living in today, you'll experience even more the healing and hope, the power and presence, the fulfillment and freedom that come when you walk with God. Growing through divorce means walking a challenging and sometimes difficult path. That path, however, is also a route of wholeness and health and abundant life in Jesus. May God bless your walk and tenderly teach you the truth of this final statement of freedom:

FREEDOM: We also glory in tribulations, knowing that tribulation produces perseverance; and perseverance, character; and character, hope. Now hope does not disappoint, because the love of God has been poured out in our hearts by the Holy Spirit who was given to us (Romans 5:3-5 NKJV).

P.S.